M000289805

Thank God for Roses

A Collection of Sweet Nothings

Rosemary Eady-West, PhD

ISBN 978-1-63874-499-3 (paperback)
ISBN 978-1-63874-500-6 (digital)

Copyright © 2021 by Rosemary Eady-West, PhD

All rights reserved. No part of this publication may be reproduced, distributed, or transmitted in any form or by any means, including photocopying, recording, or other electronic or mechanical methods without the prior written permission of the publisher. For permission requests, solicit the publisher via the address below.

Christian Faith Publishing, Inc.
832 Park Avenue
Meadville, PA 16335
www.christianfaithpublishing.com

Printed in the United States of America

To my husband Lonnie,
Thanks for allowing me to soar towards my dreams.

Contents

Gratitude

    My God 11

    Loving Him 12

    I Cry 13

    Forward..14

    I Grow Weak 15

    Flight 16

    Thankful..17

    He Smiled on Me 18

    A Rose for Your Heart 19

Praise and Worship

    Giving Myself..23

    Awakened...24

    Blessings...25

    Prayer Power 26

    Moments to Cherish 27

    Hallelujah Time 28

    Church Ways...29

Loss of Love Ones

    Your Laughter 33

    Sending Roses to Heaven 34

    Rain 35

    Lost and Found.......................................36

    Gone but Never Forgotten 37

    You're My Sunshine.................................38

    Should Have Been There..........................39

    Widow of a Buffalo Soldier 40

    My Clear Skies 41

Encouragement

    The Sky Is the Limit................................45

    Keeping My Head Up 46

    Let Your Light Shine 47

    Shining Star 48

Fall If You Must...49
If Ever I Fall 50
I'm Leaving the Lights On.................................51
Rose-Colored 52
Care for You 53
Walk Away 54
Never Stop Dreaming.......................................55
Don't Settle 56

Identity/Self Love

I Love Me Some Me 59
Mirror 60
Free 61
Me Getting to Know Me 62
Damaged..63
My Heart 64
Shifting 65
Outside Looking In 66
My Superpower..67
Best of Me..68
Got My Life Back...69
I Wish I Didn't Care...70
Something Different..71
In Spite Of..72
A Rose for a Rose 73
Keep My Feelings to Myself..............................74
My Quiet Place 75
Self-Worth..76
Full 77
Unbroken..78

Hope

Imagine..81
As One...82
Please Know Me...83
Smile Again...84
Antidote..85
Refocus on Life 86

I See Beauty 87
Stop and Smell the Roses.............................88
There's Still Hope..89
A Rose Means Forever 90

Love of Running
Running for God 93
My Fountain of Youth 94
Running Partner..95
Morning Run 96
Running for You..97
Running, Reading, and Writing 98
Sunshine 99

Dreams
Sweet Dreams...103
Daydreaming...104
Life Inside My Dreams 105
My Rose Garden 106
Mirage...107

Family
Sweet Nothings 111
Purple Flowers...112
My CC (Chocolate Child) 113
Where Did It All Go 114
My Everything Is You 115
I Want You Around 116
Merry-Go-Round..117
The Gift...118
Who Can I Run To 119

Anxiety
My Windy Days...123
Outside Pressures 124
I Wish 125
Letting Go 126
I Hurt 127
My Safe Haven..128
Sail Away...129

Nature

A Single Rose 133
Butterfly...134
Butterfly and the Rose..................................135
Rainbow...136
The Tree...137
A Description of Beauty 138
Love for the Ocean.......................................139

Gratitude

My God

Thanking, praising, and loving
My God
Dancing, singing, and shouting for
My God
Understanding, gracious, and forgiving is
My God

Loving Him

Amazing is the love of my life,
Envisioning the afterlife
Where there's no stress or strife.
Counting the seconds and minutes of the coming
And holding on to the undying promises to live
Life as we were so promised.
Amazing is the love of my life.
He's the keeper of heart and soul.
Counting the seconds and minutes of the coming
And holding on to the undying promises to live
Life as we were so promised.

I Cry

When the feelings are so strong
And words can't express
The magnitude of my emotions,
Struggling to hold it back with every breath
And every bit of my physical means,
Thinking of what repercussions I have to endure,
Just if, I cry.

Forward

I'm looking ahead and moving forward.
Ahead I go as life's trials and tribulations are displayed before me.
Hurriedly, I take each step, not realizing that my existence is being shortened.
Making decisions that dictate my destiny as I move forward,
steadying each step, ensuring that it's not repetitious of the last.
Ahead I go trying to redeem myself for mistakes made along the way.
I feel like I'm running short on time and hope to make things right.
Anxiously I set the table laying out the finest of possessions.
Pitter-patter goes my footsteps as I move forward straight into the light.
I wonder where it takes me as I move forward.

I Grow Weak

When I am praising and worshiping *you*,
Weeping and living,
Grasping and holding on to,
Modeling and displaying your word,
Reaping and appreciating the benefits,
I grow weak
When I am praising and worshiping,
Weeping and living,
Grasping and holding on to,
Modeling and displaying your word,
Reaping and appreciating the benefits,
I *love* it when
I grow weak.

Flight

Uplifted by the sweet words of my Savior,
Sun shining on my face,
Grass between my toes,
Birds singing merrily,
Rising higher and higher,
Smiling and floating through the clouds.
My body's weightless,
No burdens and worry-free.
Sounds of trumpets and beats of drums,
My flight is almost over,
Making my way home.

Thankful

Thankful I am
Strength of Samson with everlasting stamina
Knowledge and wisdom of elders
Courage of David, slaying stumbling blocks
Mesmerizing to the eyes of the beholder
Passionate to all living beings
Irrevocably in love and humbling
Grateful and thankful I am

He Smiled on Me

For my health and wealth, I am grateful
Precious Lord, I am sincerely faithful

Accomplishments and achievements, big and small
For He smiled on me through it all

With my mind stayed on Him
Hallelujah, as it says in the hymn

Focused and uplifted
Energetic and highly gifted

He smiled on me when times were rough
My standing alone was just not enough

If ever you're in need of help
Jesus is His name, just give a yelp

A Rose for Your Heart

In exchange for our hearts
He gives us roses
A multitude of roses
To nurture, then pollinate
Go forth and prosper
It's all in His plan
Reciprocal of our promise
To coexist harmoniously
Reproduce and persevere

Praise and Worship

Giving Myself

I humbly surrender myself
Me and earthly goods as well

A breathing, living sacrifice
A minimal exchange for paradise

I give my all on the altar
In this, I will never falter

Material possessions and all their value
I respectfully lay them right before you

I submit my mind, body, and soul
And everything else I can't control

All these things, I do submit
And giving my all, I shall commit

Awakened

Flowers blooming in springtime
Sweet melodies of birds
Raindrops sprinkling on my head
Gusts of winds
Sounds of sweet voices on a playground
Holding hands and making pinky promises
Soft touches on my shoulders
Waving goodbye and blowing kisses
Cherished and awakened

Blessings

Sunshine peeking through the horizon
Raindrops one by one off the rooftop
Trees budding in the gentle breeze
Birds whistling melodies of spring
Blessing, blessings in disguise

Hugs and kisses at family gatherings
Laughter and full stomachs
No room for dessert
Place setting for missing loves
Fond memories replace the hurt
Blessings, blessings in disguise

Graduations approaching soon
Plagued with emptiness
Honors and awards for such hard work
Future thoughts of things to come
Blessings, blessings in disguise

Prayer Power

Stronger than David's arm
Covered in spiritual charm

Not just words to carry us through
But expressions of thanks and praise by you

Solemn request of help or favor
Granted by God, only He can save us

An invocation of communication
Filled with passion and adoration

Anything you ask, you shall receive
If you just have faith and believe

Moments to Cherish

Inhale and smell the ever so sweet scent of wildflowers.

Stretching tall and erect toward the heavens
as beach sand and water between my toes is washed back out to sea.

Crouch down slowly and remove thorns of briars
after breathlessly running through a field.

Tremble from a fresh breeze on a wintry day
while noticing the goose pimples rise on the flesh.

Close my eyes and remember yesterday
and make a mental note of plans for tomorrow.

Thank the Almighty for all the gifts that tomorrow brings
and cherish the moments of the present.

Hallelujah Time

It's hallelujah time!
Time to shout and praise like never before,
Hallelujah!
Time to bow down and humble yourself,
Hallelujah!
Time to give thanks for all your many blessings,
Hallelujah!
Time to gift the needy,
Hallelujah!
Time to give all the glory, honor, and praise to the Almighty,
Hallelujah!

Church Ways

I love the Lord and He loves me
I sing and cry with all my heart
I praise and worship the way the spirit guides me
I believe that Jesus is the son of God and that He died for my sins
Through Him I have a direct connection to my God
Is there only one way…who is to say
I have accepted Him as my Savior
I choose to follow Him all the days of my life
He will guide me as I worship Him
In His way

Loss of Love Ones

Your Laughter

Sometimes when I'm feeling sad and blue,
Memories of your laughter get me through.

Somedays when skies are gray,
Reminiscences of your laughter make it okay.

When trouble tries to block my path,
In your laughter, I'm back on track.

All in all, what I'm trying to say,
I'll never forget your laughter; in Jesus's name, I pray.

Sending Roses to Heaven

Ascending on a massive cloud
Gently positioned and remarkably encased
In a loved one's hand
Destination bounds for the heart
Fasten seat belts and remain seated until console light comes on
Assure all electronic devices are off
Focus on the flight attendant as she demonstrates safety procedures
Roses in hand should be kept closest to the heart
Encasements sealed with a kiss
Grace and mercy honored
Showers of love permitted

Rain

It rained on me today.
My heart was heavy and blue.
I could hardly bear the weight of it.
I really miss you.
It rained on me today.
Stumbled around in a fog aimlessly.
Had you on mind.
Feelings were so heavy and so unkind.
You left me here all alone.
The rain is getting harder to bear.
Look, your picture is smiling at me.
The rain's slacking up, and my heart's getting lighter.
Your eyes told me to do it for you.
It rained on me today, and
Now in your smile, a rainbow is shining through.

Lost and Found

You left too soon
I am searching the world over
Your gone means me missing a vital part of me
This gaping hole is getting harder to repair
No bandages are strong enough to stave off the flood of sadness
I have lost my will without you
Lord, I need help to find that missing piece
Hallelujah, through you, I have found healing for my brokenness

Gone but Never Forgotten

Gone from this place
But never forgotten
Ever present is your goodness and love for us all
Only your physical presence is what's absent
Scenes of laughter and beauty
Those memories are always lingering
Gone from this place
But never forgotten
Always giving and hardly receiving
Teaching lessons that were self-taught
Because you had to learn them on your own
Gone from this place
But never forgotten
I cry for you quite often and think of how you would be
If given an equal opportunity
While sometimes things were out of your control
You made the best of your situation
You are truly loved and missed
Gone from this place
But never forgotten

You're My Sunshine

A catchy and repetitive tune
But for some, a song of gloom

Growing wings as a juvenile
Humming the tune as a child

Brightened a cloudy day
A new horizon, if I may

Ears and hearts that I sang to
Broken and hardened by it too

How could this simple melodic tune
Bring so much pain as I croon?

Memories from which it came
Still lingered, causing disdain

Putting my heart into this gift
You are my sunshine, a different twist

Should Have Been There

Living with guilt of your demise
My dreams are filled with your cries
Turn back the clock and I'd be there
To give you all my love and care
Replace you there if I could
And you'd have your life as you should
You may be looking down from heaven
But my heart still aches for your presence
Did I do enough to keep you here
Or was your time just getting near?
I'm sending roses as my token of love
And all the hugs and kisses I should have
Rest in peace, my dear beloved
And remember that you'll always be loved

Widow of a Buffalo Soldier

Doomed in darkness
Bound because of blackness
Weary days and nights
Unsecured treacherous plights
Holding on to little hope
For a better future, a slippery slope
Questioning of mere existence
And knowing it can be erased in an instance
Turning to prayer for a better future
Displays it later rather than sooner
Will my offspring survive
Or keep my legacy alive?
Will they be faced with the same?
I pray not the latter, in Jesus's name
Will this cold world change its heart?
Will it spiral into hell before I depart?
Hosanna, Hosanna, you're here to save me
In your name, I'll walk the life you gave me
Carrying with me a beautiful rose
All fear and doubt rest in repose

My Clear Skies

Days when the hurt is gone from me
When you're just a distant memory

Appear my clear skies with no clouds or rain
Just enough to take away the pain

Sunny and bright for miles and miles
Coupled with my beaming smiles

I forget about feelings of sorrow
Looking ahead at skies of tomorrow

No more sadness and hopeless cries
No more lonely gray skies

If thoughts of you invade my day
My clear skies will frighten them away

Encouragement

The Sky Is the Limit

Said often as to motivate excellence
Imagine succeeding its limitless heights
To go where no one has gone before
Spiritual form only is this worthy flight
Welcome aboard the flight into your future
It is the ride of a lifetime
Determined by choices made on your time
Ascend as we must because no stops can be made
No standard distance added to this crusade
So plan and plan carefully
To sow the seeds and reap completely

Keeping My Head Up

Ain't gonna cry no more,
Ain't gonna crawl no more.

Gonna push harder,
Gonna work smarter.

Gotta stand up straight,
Gotta get my mind right.

Gotta look up,
Gotta keep my head up!

Let Your Light Shine

Don't cover up or withdraw into your shell
Because you matter and have so much to tell

Put your war clothes on and join the fight
Speak up allowing all your inner self to take flight

Little do you know, but you're a gem
Glistening and sparkly compared to them

Don't be shy or shortchange your worth
He has a plan for you given at birth

No looking down or dragging your feet
There's nothing wrong with marching to your own beat

Climb your mountain to the top
And blessings will come nonstop

When your work and His way align
It'll be easier to let your light shine

Shining Star

A twinkle from the highest
Showing yourself at its best

With everything that you possess
Time to take the test

Remember that you're a star
Shining brightly from afar

Never ever second-guess
Don't forget that you are blessed

Show your beauty and watch it gleam
Loveliness and goodness on full beam

Shine, shine, star, for all to see
This is what is meant to be

Fall If You Must

Headed in the wrong direction
Destructive and misguided decisions

Near misses and close encounters
Shouts and cries for help seem louder

Fall if you must, for I am here to pick up
Your broken and shattered cup

Steering unsteadily with no regards
For damages or hurt to self and others

Please slow down and gather your thoughts
My cleanups are getting tedious and come at a loss

Fall if you must, but please understand that each time you fail
It's a reflection on me and my legacy to no avail

If Ever I Fall

I know that you will have my back
That includes my slipping through the crack

Surely I'm not planning on making a fall
Sometimes champions can hit a wall

Reaching the top, a tremendous feat
But it doesn't take much to get knocked off your feet

If ever I fall with my belly scraping the ground
I pray that you'll be somewhere close or hanging around

I'll do my best to stay on a straight, narrow path
As I was taught, what a daunting task

Rest assured that I'd do likewise for you
For in my heart, it's what I'm supposed to do

Again, I'm not planning on making a fall
Just trying to make sure you're there when I call

I'm Leaving the Lights On

Fly away and spread your wings
Can't wait to see what your future brings

Forever welcome to come and go
You've plenty of seeds to plant and sow

Commit to Him in all you say or do
And you shall prosper in all you pursue

Like open arms they'll be a light
To guide you back home through the night

So climb your mountains to the top
Reach your potential, giving honor to God

Forever leaving a light on
To guide you back home

Rose-Colored

Cold, cold world void of emotions
Temporarily stagnant and broken

I see brightly hued colors
Of people loving each other

Through rose-colored lenses
With evidence of my senses

What sometimes seems unlikely
Are answered prayers to put it politely

Also, peace and harmony
And God-given liberty

Through rose-colored lenses
A new beginning to cleanse us

Grateful I am to have this vision
To repent of sins and be forgiven

Care for You

Feel free to fly with broken wings
Endure all that it brings

That day on Calvary
It was done for you and me

Reparations were submitted
Although bloodshed was committed

Stumble in your attempts to succeed
In all your heart you mustn't concede

Remain strong in your walk with truth
And in arm's reach there's care for you

Walk Away

After trying to make things right
Ignoring temptation to get into a fight
Walk away
Exchanges of words that could hurt you
Emotions too strong to help divert you
Walk away
When reasoning falls on deaf ears
Not accepting logic brings about tears
Walk away
When earlier it was just a squabble
Turn the other cheek is what's in the Bible
Walk away

Never Stop Dreaming

Off on an escapade
Needing an escape

Dreams somehow out of view
Discouragement hinders pursuit

Searching for inner strength
To recreate dreams within

With His will, it all seems possible
Your might and drive are unstoppable

Never let go of your visions
Or use someone else's decisions

Stand firm by your own intuitions
And all your dreams will come to fruition

Don't Settle

No don't settle for less than you're worth
Deserving of the best always inferred

Spread your wings to the fullest
Temptations cause you to resist
Or settle for second best

No, don't settle into mediocre
Prove to be much smarter

Success is for your grabbing
All that it entails is worth having
Someday you'll look back

And smile and sometimes laugh
At decisions good and bad

No, don't settle for less than you're worth
Accept his plan given to you at birth

Prove to yourself that anything you work for
Shines bright and produce a mighty score

Identity/Self Love

I Love Me Some Me

I just love my intellect essential in any challenging task
I love my resilience and stamina
Capability to overcome and overthrow if need be
I love my hard-core exterior but gentleness applied to given
circumstances
Competence and commitment to matters at hand
I love my thoughtfulness and patience when warranted
Complexion, curves, and kinky hair
I love my big eyes and full lips
I just love me some me!

Mirror

A reflection of myself in the mirror
Shows my life even clearer

Trying hard to be more like Jesus
Emulating of how he sees us

Beholding him and transforming into his likeness
And focus on his benevolent brightness
Mirror his labor and means of righteousness

I must mirror his work and his ways
To be born again before the end of days

Free

I'm afraid of how it always makes me feel
I have to get out and coalesce
My hair is different
My skin is different
The people I look like say I sound different
Where do I fit in
I just want to be free
Free to look, dress, and talk like me
Whom do I please
Will I ever be accepted
Should I go on as is
Or try to change
If I change, I'll never be free
Because it won't be *me*

Me Getting to Know Me

Introverted and soft-spoken is what they say
I keep wondering, am I really that way?

Spiritually gifted a servant's heart
And willing to help from the start

Who am and why am I so special
All I do is what comes natural

This gift of mine delves deep inside my soul
I guess it's the key to making me whole

I appreciate those kind words and thoughts
Of doing what comes natural at no cost

Damaged

Goods fragile and broken
Born into sin hardly a token

Promises to set things straight
With hands on the lever that opens the gate

Although spoiled and surely ruined
I know God can get me through it

In all my cries for help and sorrow
The sun will always shine tomorrow

Confessions of sin or iniquities
Will grant forgiveness and life eternally

My Heart

So pure and fragile
Under lock and key

Gates cannot be breached
It's guarded heavily

My heart doesn't know that emotions fade
The feelings stay strong as it withers and become frayed

How will it know when to stop
It won't, is the reason my walls will not just drop

Listen and hear me now
Protecting it forever I will vow

Shifting

This is ever present and takes place naturally
Although it can be done when necessary
Trending are norms and cliques that inhabit humanity
These past, present, and future behaviors are here to stay
Shifting allows one a certain belonging
It permits participation in sacred activities not offered to all
Watch me as I go places traveled by a select group
I'm not a member, nor do I hold a special invitation
I'm just playing the game in the game of life that I was born into
Who wrote the rules that keep certain people out
What exactly are the criteria
I have paid my dues and put in all the hard work
When will I be able to fit in without shifting outside of me
Lord, please help us...shifting back and forth is wasting me

Outside Looking In

I see something beautiful
Something broken and hurt
Something strong and resilient
Something honest and compassionate
Something kind and generous
Something unselfish and loyal
Something intelligent and clever
Something energetic and optimistic
Something made in His image
I see something beautiful
Outside looking in

My Superpower

Singing is something I don't take for granted
My audiences say I leave them enchanted

This gift I have is not a priority
Compared to others, I feel there is inferiority

For years, I've been pushed to sing solos
Maybe they see something better, I suppose

Minister to those who may need healing or just to inspire
Ability to send a message on things that transpire

Just carrying a tune is how I see it
A superpower in disguise, I must admit

Best of Me

Not perfect or even close
It's my best, not wanting to boast
Superseded all goals that were set
The last was the best one yet
For my all is the best of me
A gift from God bestowed upon me
The mountainous journey taken step-by-step
Valleys, rivers with some missteps
Resilience to withstand a mighty storm
And majestic oceans rush without harm
For my all is the best of me
A gift from God bestowed upon me
A collection of scars from triumphs
Merely badges of courage not symptoms
No weapons can take my victory
And with Him none will conquer me
For my all is the best of me
A gift from God bestowed upon me

Got My Life Back

All the joy and happiness
Replaced by craziness.
You hijacked my heart,
Never ever minutes apart.
How I allowed such misery,
Oh Lord, is beyond me.
Here's a note, a matter of fact,
I got my life back.

Robbed of laughs and fun times,
Most days rainy with no sunshine,
Tear-soaked pillows and swollen eyes,
All day inside, no surprise,
I got my life back in time,
And I'm leaving bad memories behind.

Increased my faith and will to live
My life and perhaps forgive
The bondage you inflicted,
And your spells are all lifted.
I thank the Lord that I'm back.
Yes, I'm on the right track.

I Wish I Didn't Care

Background noise that's discouraging
Mere morsels in comparison
To all that's encouraging
I wish I didn't care, but I do!
Looks that show unacceptance
Inflicting discrimination and prejudices
Tolerance and silence
Of behaviors that aren't personal
I wish I didn't care, but I do!
Inhale, exhale while representation of me
Is hardly visible
How is that possible, almost invisible?
Futuristic plans do not include me
Others overrun it as far as I can see.
I wish I didn't care, but I do!
Time to speak louder
Stand up taller
And put it in the hands of my Beholder!

Something Different

Morphing to make a better fit
Present image not satisfied with

Perception of one by others can hurt
The self-perception of an introvert

Longing to be something you're not
Leopards shouldn't change its spots

Insecurities and feelings are strong
An unexplained urging that I don't belong

Pulling and pushing
Bending and twisting
Into something different

Yes, I do, I do belong!
My God says there's nothing wrong

Fearfully and wonderfully made
A precious work of art displayed

In Spite Of

Brick walls of rejections
And diagnosed infections

Overcame boundaries of redwoods
Climbed hills I didn't think I could

Immeasurable fortitude and the right attitude
Brought gifts of the highest magnitude

Succumbed then conquered
Temptations that hindered

In spite of all the setbacks and drawbacks
My diligence and perseverance begat rewards and kind acts

A Rose for a Rose

Beautiful
Innocent
Passionate
Enthusiastic
Pure
Loyal
Graceful
Joyous
Perfection
Love
And prickly

Keep My Feelings to Myself

Love stronger than the tallest trees
And the sweetest honey from bees
But I'm keeping my feelings to myself

Vulnerability it will display
Can't have you see me that way
Sadness plagues my heart
In hurtful situations we depart
A shot through tears us apart
Still blinded by love
Trouble gets a shove
So I'm keeping my feelings to myself

This hurt you'll never witness
In fear that it will finish us
I love you today more than ever
I've forgotten about all the drama
Will I explode
Or gradually implode
By keeping my feelings to myself

My Quiet Place

There's no place I'd rather be
Than my own sitting quietly

No fuss or fright
To my delight

Just me in this perfect space
Covered in God's grace

Graphic thoughts and dreams
All my own, so it seems

No interruptions or traps
Holding on to hope, perhaps

It's okay to visit this place
My private personal space

In the corners of my mind
To get away from a world so unkind

Self-Worth

Do I measure up?
Can I take on the responsibilities before me?
Will I be able to endure the storms?
Am I competent, or will my works speak for me?
Let all your gifts be gifts unexpectedly
Bringing hope to hopeless, but
Upwardly hold your own worth
Into branches that extend toward your merit
Never diminish your gifts
Shine bright for the unworthiness
Take a flight spreading across the vast sky
Conveying love, warmth, and tenderness and
Remembering through it all
Love yourself is the greatest of gifts

Full

I am so full
Of love and life
Overflowing with the sweet perfume of love
Handing out fliers along the way
A beacon brightly shining in every path
Infectious and liberating beautiful thoughts and wisdom
Piling up and diffusing naturally
Gratitude and appreciation to the Almighty

Unbroken

Though born in sin
In his image unbroken

Resilient like the ocean waters
As strong as mountains before us

Although I am slightly damaged
Thankful and never taken for granted
Beautiful and obedient

Flaws and imperfections
I am gratefully unbroken

Hope

Imagine

Eyes on His face
In that heavenly place
Tears of joy and grace
Open arms to embrace
Heart love filled and impassioned
Just imagine if this happened
Weakness with emotions
Most powerful of potions
Praise from the most high, the one
Just to say a job well done
Eager to earn that praise
To live and work in his grace
My all and everything is you
Giving honor, glory, and praise to You
To be in your presence, I'd be honored
On my knees, I humble myself
Pouring of my heart in prayers
To only imagine this perfect greet
To exist and bow at Your feet

As One

Can we become intertwined
And accepting of each other's minds

Differences and beliefs
Agree to live life harmoniously

God made us in His own image
Visually different but part of His lineage

Strip away plans of privileges
Love each other as He encourages

Teach our children to love no matter what
Or will we continue on in this rut

As they learn from our Savior
Maybe we can learn from their behavior

As one the world can be a better place
Only if our differences we learn to embrace

Please Know Me

Who am I?
Will you get to know me?
Can you even see me?
Am I important?
Will my merit be enough?
What more can I do?
Please know me?
Please like me?
I am a child of God too.

Smile Again

Heartache from a vision
A world filled with civil unrest
Conspiracy a causation of division
Refusal to compromise
Can we just smile again?

Headaches and breathless
Trying to wish it all away
Prayers seem unanswered
Facing dangerous situations
Can we just smile again?

Wanting peace and dreaming of a perfect world
Overcoming the heartache
And feelings of doom
Change will come soon
Because it's God's will
And smile again, we will!

Antidote

Strong and potent is required
We are so tired

Do it like this, not like that
How can we keep on track

When we stand up
We get kicked out of the club

What will it take
For heaven's sake

To cure the hate
Is this our fate

Give us an antidote at last
Unlike those that have forepassed

Refocus on Life

Dial it back and refocus
Decrease all that replaces your focus

Concentrate on self and mind
Stop running away all the time
Center of balance a must find

Dial it back and refocus
Seek that which woke us
And has put us on notice

Receive positivity that's given
Reject and don't give in

To negativity and despair
No more than we can bear

Is God's promise to us
Remember to dial it back and refocus

I See Beauty

A squirrel scampering across the lawn hurriedly gathering nuts to store,
Bees buzzing and headed for landing on a delicate rose petal,
An ant bed awakens by the jittery squirrel gathering nuts,
Beautiful work of God is what I see.

Drops of dew perfectly arranged on the rose petals,
Sounds of sprinklers watering the grassy lawns,
The sweet smell of morning and the quietness thereof,
Beautiful work of God is what I see.

The warmth of the sun piercing through the clouds,
Pit-a-pat of a jogger's feet on a morning run,
Children giggling as they walk to their school bus stop,
Beautiful work of God is what I see.

Stop and Smell the Roses

Always rushing,
Always running,
Gotta go to work.

Always jumping,
Always hopping,
Gotta take care of my family.

Always helping,
Always giving,
Never got a minute to spare.

Always exhausting,
Always hurting,
Gotta slow down.

Always alluring,
Always aromatizing,
Gotta smell the roses.

There's Still Hope

The chirping of baby birds on a spring morning,
Sunlight beaming through my window, and
The smell of freshly brewed coffee is what gives me hope.
Children playing on a playground, singing nursery rhymes,
A young man holding the door or
Giving up his seat for an elder is what gives me hope.
People of different races agreeing and standing
up for what's right by God,
Not silence or submission or looking the
other way when there's harm or
Mistreatment, lets me know there's still hope.

A Rose Means Forever

Souls don't lie
Emotionally drawn into a web of feelings
Trying to figure out this journey
Blood red fragile petals
Resilient and unwavering
Thorns of intense moods leading to more and more
Entombed thankfully and wittingly
Questions of faithfulness put to rest

Love of Running

Running for God

A quest for deeper understanding
Simple pleasure that's demanding
Faithfulness requires ambition
Like running a race is competition
A straight race is to commit
Selfless love and devotion depicts
Inhale, exhale journey toward my goal
Uphill, downhill heart and soul
Running a never-ending race
Seeking that heavenly place
To lay eyes upon His face
Open arms graciously embrace
Eternal resting space
Temperature and pressure rising
With a quickened pulse spiking
Steadily turning the corner
Making my way to the altar

My Fountain of Youth

With God's grace I've found my fountain of youth
No charge
No requirements
Just don my running attire
No deadline
No prerequisites
Just willpower and fortitude
To transcend the many challenges of life
With God's grace I've found my fountain of youth
No stress
No invitation
The most natural movement since infancy
In solo or accompanied
With frequency comes impulse that
Result in youthfulness and longevity
With God's grace I've found my fountain of youth

Running Partner

I cherish my running partner
A tranquil scene almost breathless and speechless in each mile
Encouraged to push harder as the GPS time expires
No need to see You
Because You're omnipresent
Omnipotent and omniscient
And an entirely omnibenevolent being
Always equipped to run the course with me
Completing it in its entirety

Morning Run

Feeling so fine
Smells of honeysuckles piercing the air
Sweet smells of roses in full bloom
Drops of dew melting in the beautiful sunlight
My soul laughs as I put one foot in front of the other
Palpitations rush as it skips a beat
Wind tickling my nose
Feeling so fine
Back straight, don't slump
Arms above the waist
One mile, two miles, three
'Bout to reach my destiny
Feeling so fine

Running for You

Wake up, hurry up, and excited
Dressed and stringing up my shoes
Coffee, music, and out the door
I love it! Can't get enough of it!
Weather isn't always good, deal with it
Sometimes painful, push through
Oh, my knees, my back, my hip
Torturous, satisfying, calming, and addictive
I love it! Can't get enough of it!
Why? Why do I engage in this affair, this ritual?
Is it for them or you?
Who are they and who are you?
I got it! The *you* is me!
I love it! Can't get enough of it!
Running for you, yay!

Running, Reading, and Writing

My true loves are unified in all respects
Running for you, Lord
Fortify my body a temple, train
Of the Holy Spirit within me
Reading for you, Lord
Protection of the mind and its power, shield
Ensure that it aligns with God's promise
Writing for you, Lord
Covered by His blood, transcribe
My pen is guided in His way
True love's different but inspired by same principles

Sunshine

I can feel its warmness and beauty
Grateful and motivated
The neighborhood's mostly still asleep
Sweat slowly forms on my forehead
Heartbeat rapidly plays in my ear along with music from my playlist
I feel like dancing and shouting
No pain or stiffness, just pure bliss
I'm smiling from ear to ear
Waving at the dog walkers and people leaving for work
I'm feeling thankful and blessed
Beauty is fully displayed through me and the sunshine as I run
All God's glory and grace is shining through

Dreams

Sweet Dreams

Lanky palm trees strewn elegantly
Vivid blue water swish to meet the sand
Radiant moments of warmness
Sun-scorched, bronzed skin
Salty to the touch and sweat-bathed
Hues of the sky just right
Cirrus clouds randomly scattered
In casually shaped hearts overlapping
And you sitting right here beside me

Daydreaming

Sadness often invades my dreams
Of you and what it would mean

If I could still see you smile
And feel your presence for awhile

The pain hovers sometimes in length
Slowly and ever so tense

Clear skies and sunshine change the scene
Making it feel more than only a dream

Your laughter and singing so vividly serene
Eagerness I feel just to stay in this dream

Hallelujah to the Almighty for these moments with you
My moments grow stronger and I'm not feeling blue

Life Inside My Dreams

Life is beautiful inside my dreams
Leaving behind all the troubles, it seems

I wish that I could fall asleep one day
And automatically make everything okay

I'm not wishing for my demise
Just the changes that I see inside

Where all is well and life is good
All intended like He said it should

Outside hurt and hate is too much
With feelings of hopelessness and such

If my dreams and life one day coincide
My God in the highest will be glorified

My Rose Garden

A place that's diverse
With an array of colors and hues
Various species one no more beautiful than the other
Tenderly handled with love and care
Cultivated soil to enhance potential
Attention dispersed equally
Pruned and praised with room to bloom
Protection to deter life's infestations
Guidance to promote a healthier duration
A budding rose garden revealing a variety of blossoms

Mirage

While searching for that visual of paradise
Scenes of intangible miracles yet enough to mesmerize

The place we often visit in the corners of our mind
So vivid and mystical a treasure to all mankind

Though flowing with milk, honey, and a pearly gate
We are the architects of our own fate

If we're headed down the wrong track
Making mistakes back-to-back

The mirage we seek may appear quite often
But in fact, it is just a precaution

Family

Sweet Nothings

I found the roses you gave me on our first date
Safely tucked away in my Bible
Although flattened and aged, the possession
of beauty and love is still evident
Filled the vase with water that held the roses
you gave me on our first date
Missing was the roses and their aromatic presence
Yet a vision of finely carved crystal
Nothing is sweeter than metaphors of the
roses that filled that beautiful vase
A memento of our first date

Purple Flowers

It's her favorite color
I really miss her
Daydreaming of the color purple
And running through a field of lavender
Barefooted and free
Smells so sweet,
Tranquil and breezy
I feel her here with me
These flowers I give her
Are many shades of purple
I miss my dear mother
I'm sending kisses to heaven
Because of the gifts she's given
As she looks down from above
I hope she feels unconditional love

My CC (Chocolate Child)

Deep cocoa skin
Filled with melanin

And eyes that smile
She's my chocolate child

Athletic and scholarly
A carbon copy of me

When old enough to speak
She'd echo, I am a CC

Are you a chocolate child, she'd murmur
When others seemed to look like her

It is how she was referred to
Nothing negative or cruel

Just describing her beauty
And embracing it gladly

Where Did It All Go

From giggles to singing,
Childhood games and pinky promising,
Where'd it all go?
Late-night talks about growing up,
College and getting married up,
The number of children
And husbands or boyfriends,
Where'd it all go?
Sisterly conversations at bedtime
About everything that came to mind,
Mama yelling for us to go to bed
Lowering our voices with all that we said,
Where'd it all go?
Ironing school clothes for the next day,
Homework and before closing our eyes to pray,
Sweet dreams of future life
In hopes that there's no stress or strife,
Where'd it all go?
Into lessons of life as we know
That helped us to learn and to grow

My Everything Is You

You are my reason
My life, love, and worth even

Waking up each day
Thoughts of you, bae

Strengthens my existence
In every circumstance and condition

I hold on because of you
Otherwise, my world is through

Hosanna, you saved me
To live life abundantly

You answered my prayers
Gave me someone who cares

Everything, everything is you
Everything and all that I do
I graciously extend thanks to you

I Want You Around

You're needed every day of my life
It's an honor to be your wife

Different opinions and thoughts
That gel together like a secret sauce

Sometimes when skies are gray
And rain shows up that day
The sun appears to dry it all away

Your love for God and his way
Is our main ingredient, I pray

Take care of your health and physical means
So that having you around is not just a dream

Merry-Go-Round

Round and round is how the ride goes.
My ticket was rejected as I watched others board.
Is it a ride of privilege or entitlement?

Spiraling and spiraling into frenzies of mindlessness,
I feel left out and wonder should I try again.
Did I do something wrong or right?

Spinning and spinning out of control,
My ticket was rejected as I watch loved ones and friends board.
I wonder is it a ride of pleasure or consequences?

Twirling and twirling as a tumbleweed into a ball of lifelessness.
Suddenly, I fall to my knees, humbling myself
and praising the only way I know how.
This merry-go-round was a ride I rejected with the choices I made.

My ticket was not rejected.
Thank you, God, in Jesus's name, amen!

The Gift

Out of breath and soaking wet, I awake with
Vivid details of laughter, joy, pain, and
sometimes tragedy on my mind.
My only thought is how to relay these messages to those involved.
The gift to convey the scenarios of emotions
sometimes mirrors a curse.
Should I be the bearer of bad news, or shall
I pick and choose the messages
Of laughter and joy to only share?
My heart aches as I visit a loved one in what seems like the last time.
Tears flow and swollen red eyes are symptoms of the tragedy in what
Felt like a dream or was it a daydream.
Is this a gift or a curse, or is this a superpower
that hasn't come to fruition?
Smiling, singing, and dancing to a beautiful feeling that's uplifting,
Eager to call and share,
It's not so bad when the news to bare is beneficial to share.

Who Can I Run To

Who will take away the pain
When my life is filled with rain?

Who will erase memories of hate
And wrongdoings that seem like fate?

Who can I run to and cry on their shoulder?
The state of my existence is getting colder and colder.

Who will hold my hand,
As I try to take a stand?

Who can I run to and help make a change?
Wanting to make a difference is not so strange.

Whose love for me is greater than my own?
Who said He'd never let me walk alone?

Who already knew from the start
That He'd always be with me and never depart?

Anxiety

My Windy Days

Like the wind, my feelings change directions
Up, down, left, right, anxiety or depression

Staggering to stay afoot
Uncontrollably obscure

Guided by my own decisions
And words that are true collisions

Whichever way the wind blows
Or what the day brings, who knows?

Drowning in a whirlwind of emotions
Teeming and as continuous as the ocean

Sometimes cold, other times not
Smothered deeply into a thickened plot

Praying for peace and settlement
My windy days are such torment

Looking to the hills, I'll just keep looking to the hills
From whence my help shall be revealed

Outside Pressures

Hands on my head
To relieve this pressure

Misguided directions
Coming from all over

Implosion seems very likely
Are there any others like me?

Feelings of distress
Growing harder to suppress

Heavenly Father, I'm praying for relief
Ask and receive is my belief

Keeper of my heart and soul
Restful and refreshing in his control

I bow my head and fall to my knees
Our walk into eternity is how he's most pleased

I Wish

I wish I had the mesmerizing beauty of a waterfall
Alluring to all whose gaze is fortunate to befall

I wish I had the strength of a mountain standing tall
Whose magnificence overshadows and protects all

I wish I possessed the freedom of water rushing back out to sea
Sometimes predictable but mostly free

I wish I could save the world from all that ails it
The power to supply the needs and erase everything that fails it

I wish I had knowledge to right all that's wrong
My faith in His power I continue to keep strong

He is the answer to all my wishes
All-knowing, seeing, and hearing, He is

Letting Go

Sadness and heartache
How much more can I take

Everything is so contrived
I have to let go to survive

Relinquish the pain, I surmise
Holding on will only delay

What's in store for me today
I'm letting go because I know

I'm not perfect
Or if it's worth it

I have to fulfill my purpose
To do all things in the name of Jesus

I Hurt

When there's hunger and famine
When there's pain and sickness
When there's suicides and homicides
When there's lying and cheating
When there's crying in the street for equality and justice for all
When there's division and exclusion
When it seems like there's no resolution
When we forget about His promise for a better tomorrow
I hurt

My Safe Haven

I love this place
It's secure and safe

Doors open whenever I need
Protection from harm guaranteed

Uncomfortably thought of
But a place of love

A place so familiar but yet foreign
A gift from the most gracious, He's sovereign

The Lord's voice sharing it with me
Son of God, please have mercy

Not a dark space, my safe haven,
And it feels like heaven.

Sail Away

Royal blue and glossy
Glide across the sea
Take me from it all
Sorry to leave y'all
Give me a minute
It'd be for everyone's benefit
Time to refocus
It will only strengthen us
Waters smooth and serene
Blue skies to match the scene
Alone with my thoughts
And God with whom I talk
Taking a set at the table
Prepared as in the Bible
To sail away in His words
Will cure all that hurts
Away, oh yes, I must sail
To breathe in and exhale

Nature

A Single Rose

Splendor captures the heart
Vibrant petals for each part

Alluring scent blowing in the breeze
Entrances prey, please don't sneeze

Precision-cut precious gem
Prickly extended stem

Perfection and highly prized
A rare jewel of paradise

Butterfly

Flutters with poise and grace
Strut your beauty and embrace
Newfound elegance and life
Symbolic of resurrection
Rebirth and transformation
Strength in your significance
A wondrous and supernatural task
Indicative of things to come

Butterfly and the Rose

Oh me, oh my, oh me, oh my
Magically fluttering gracefully by

Proudly show us your new you
Perfection and courageous too

Searching for that landing site
A beautiful rose, oh what a delight

Rose, rose, don't you fret
This marriage made in heaven best thing yet

Rainbow

Colorful and brilliant I must confess
A bridge that connects us to success
Arched above for all to see
Is your presence just for me?
Do others see you as do I?
Strewn across the heavenly sky
Were you sent to tell a story
Of things to come and all its glory
Speak, speak to give us our fortune
Your puzzling mystery is a torture
Maybe you're here to bring good luck
Or answer to a problem that's too tough
Your beautifully array of colors
Lined perfectly to complement each other
Regardless the reason
Or whatever else happens
Your existence ceased the rain
Presenting sunlight once again

The Tree

Seedling pure and innocent
Vulnerable to all earth's inhabitants
Accepting of a wealth of experiences
When fertilized and irrigated
Reproduction provides multitudes of favor
Its glory and grace extend beyond its static position
As it reaches its full potential
Roots entrenched and planted firmly
Branches outstretched enough to feed a nation
Fruits of labor to go forth
And reproduce as seeds of its self
Consequences and rewards granted contingent on growth
Through its trials and tribulations
Its likeness to Jesus is astonishing

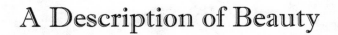

A Description of Beauty

A sound,
A smell,
A vision,
A feeling,
Indescribable,
Inexpressible,
Indefinable,
And very subtle

Love for the Ocean

Its beauty and innocence,
Mesmerizing sounds that capture my heart,
Massive waves cool, captivating and fluid,
It won't judge or turn me away.
I live for it every day.
I love it, and I know this,
The ocean I will always treasure in every way.

About the Author

Rosemary Eady-West is an accomplished scholar, educator, military service member, and now she can add published author to her repertoire. Her life has been lived as one that is representative of a true servant's heart. She has been very intentional about using her God-given gifts in constant service of others for the greater good.

Dr. Eady-West was born in Georgia and raised between Florida and Georgia. Her formal education of being a lifelong learner includes receiving an AA degree in 1981. She continued her studies on a track-and-field and basketball scholarships. She earned her BA in education in 1984. In 1999, she completed her MEd degree in integrated education. In 2017, with God's perfect grace, she successfully defended her dissertation and was awarded her PhD in education from Capella University in Minneapolis, Minnesota.

Dr. Eady-West proudly served in the United States Army Reserves as an enlisted service member, as a drill sergeant, and an officer for twenty-seven years, wherein she retained the rank of captain, until her retirement in 2015. Simultaneously, in the civilian sector, Dr. Eady-West was a teacher and coach for thirty-four years until her retirement in 2019.

Dr. Eady-West currently resides in Northeast Florida with her husband, Lonnie, for twenty-six years. She is enjoying her hobbies of reading, writing short stories, running, and spending time with her family and friends. Even in retirement, she continues to attempt to make the world a better place by spreading a message of encouragement to her readers to be strong in faith and love, to live life like that of a rose—even as it grows among thorns, the rose maintains its grandeur.

CPSIA information can be obtained
at www.ICGtesting.com
Printed in the USA
BVHW071513131221
623924BV00002B/182